HAWAI'I VOLCANOES

NATIONAL PARK

FIRE FROM BENEATH
THE SEA

BY
BARBARA DECKER
AND
ROBERT DECKER

SIERRA PRESS
MARIPOSA, CA

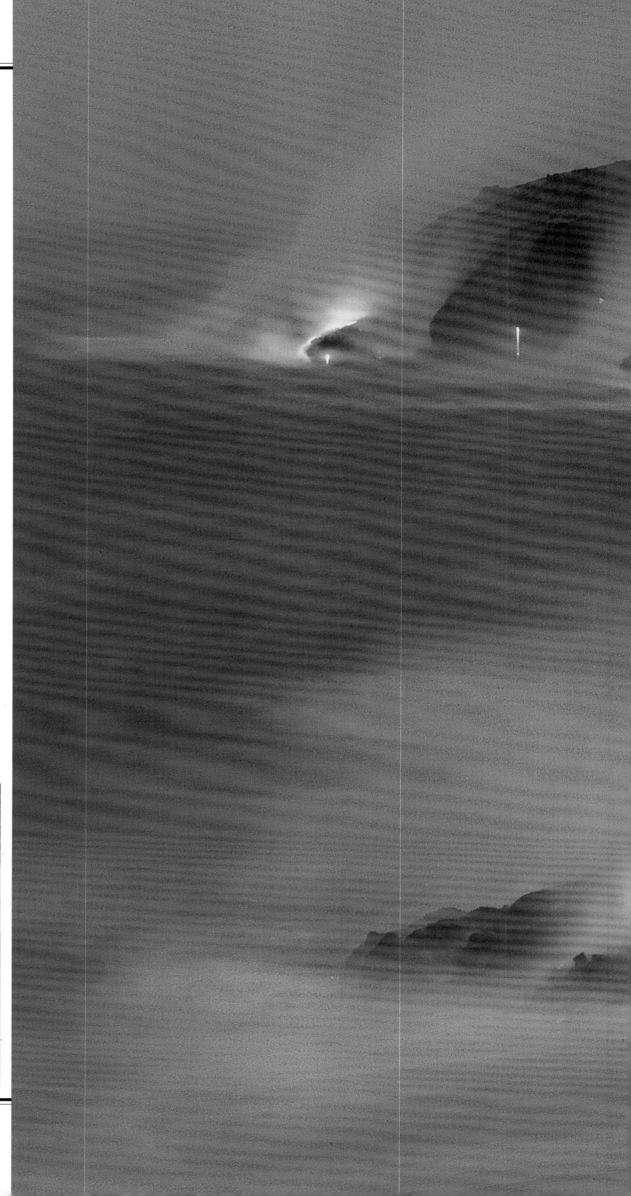

ACKNOWLEDGMENTS

Special thanks to Kathy English and Margot Griffith of Hawai'i Natural History Association and Superintendent Jim Martin, Jim Quiring, James Gale, Mardie Lane, and Bobby Camara of Hawai'i Volcanoes National Park as well as Linda Pratt and Thane Pratt of the United States Geological Survey—not to mention all the talented photographers who made their imagery available for use in this book.   —JDN

FRONT COVER
Lava flowing into the Pacific Ocean.
PHOTO© MICHAEL T. STEWART
INSIDE FRONT COVER
Aerial view of Pu'u 'Ō'ō vent, Kīlauea.
PHOTO© MICHAEL T. STEWART
TITLE PAGE
Lava erupting, Kīlauea. USGS PHOTO BY J.D. GRIGGS
PAGE 4 (BELOW)
Morning glory on pāhoehoe lava.
PHOTO© LARRY ULRICH
PAGE 4/5
Lava from Kīlauea flowing into sea.
PHOTO© MICHAEL T. STEWART
PAGE 6/7
Hāpu'u (tree ferns) and 'ōhi'a lehua along the Kīlauea Iki Trail. PHOTO© LARRY ULRICH
PAGE 7 (LOWER RIGHT)
Pāhoehoe lava engulfing tree.
PHOTO© MICHAEL T. STEWART

CONTENTS

INTRODUCTION TO HAWAI'I

Lava falls between two lake levels, Kīlauea's Mauna Ulu eruption, 1972.
USGS PHOTO BY R.T. HOLCOMB

Before we could see the lava flow, we could feel its heat and hear the noise of trees breaking and crashing to the ground as the thick wall of molten rock moved through the forest above us. Lava from Kīlauea Volcano's east rift zone was threatening the remote Royal Gardens subdivision just outside Hawai'i Volcanoes National Park, and scientists were there to monitor its course.

There was still some hope that this flow might follow the path of an earlier one and miss the upper corner of the subdivision, but just at dusk as we watched in awe a huge, glowing mass of lava moved slowly out of the dense 'ōhi'a forest and overran the top of Queen Avenue. This was a massive, chunky flow of a type of lava that geologists call 'a'ā, and it advanced more slowly than would the thinner, more liquid pāhoehoe lava. About six feet thick, this jumble of red-orange molten rock had an upper crust that had cooled to black; it inched forward about two feet a minute with red-hot rocks cascading and clinking down the steep front of the flow. Moving slowly but inexorably, it toppled and burned blooming 'ōhi'a trees, tall tree ferns, and mango trees heavy with ripening fruit. Every few minutes we heard small underground explosions as far as 100 yards from the edges of the flow as heated tree roots gave off gas that suddenly ignited with a loud thud, tossing fist-sized rocks high into the air.

While we walked slowly downhill in front of the advancing flow, we noticed that it had gradually increased in thickness to an impressive twenty feet and was starting to move more rapidly. With a growing roar the hot flow suddenly surged forward, crossed Tuberose Street, and completely engulfed a two-story house, crushing and burning it as easily as a cardboard box. In less than two minutes the yard was a pile of steaming black rock, with no suggestion that a house had ever stood there.

This was the first home destroyed in the long-lasting Pu'u 'Ō'ō eruption of Kīlauea Volcano, but unfortunately not the last. Some homeowners in the path of the flows surrounded their houses with offerings to appease Pele, the Hawaiian Goddess of volcanoes; bunches of ti leaves, as well as hopeful but non-traditional gifts of plumeria lei and, in at least one driveway, a bottle of gin. She

accepted some of the offerings and ignored others. Since 1983, lava flows have claimed 184 buildings, an ancient Hawaiian heiau (temple), a National Park Visitor Center, and thousands of acres of native forest. Small wonder that the folktales of people in volcanic areas all over the world tell of a huge beast emerging from a forest to devour a village.

But in spite of all this, eruptions in Hawai'i seldom take a toll in human life. As volcanoes go, Kīlauea and her larger sister Mauna Loa are considered "quiet"; that is to say, they generally do not have explosive eruptions like those at Mount St. Helens, Krakatau, and other notoriously deadly volcanoes. Quiet was not the word that came to mind, though, the first time we were lucky enough to see the beginning of one of Kīlauea's eruptions. The combination of the shaking ground, the jet-like roar of the lava fountains, the sulphurous smell and radiant heat from the molten lava, and the stunning sight of fountains of fire playing sometimes 1,500 feet in the air and falling into lakes of glowing lava make it an experience rather than a show.

At 340 square miles, Hawai'i Volcanoes National Park is large—especially for an island park, but that figure is subject to change. Since late 1986, streams of lava from the Pu'u 'Ō'ō eruption have flowed down Kīlauea's flanks—often in lava tubes but sometimes in surface flows—on their way to the coast. There the glowing streams pour over sea cliffs into the ocean sending steam plumes high into the air, and adding new land to the island. Since 1986, 510 acres have been added to the Island of Hawai'i—the newest land on Earth. As anyone who lives in volcano country can tell you, the cycle of destruction and renewal is the natural order.

Since the park extends from sea level to more than 13,000 feet at the top of Mauna Loa you can see all stages of the cycle: new land forming at the coast, glistening new lava fields, tiny islands of life where plants are starting to colonize, and humid tropical rainforests growing on ancient flows. At a higher elevation the mysterious Ka'ū Desert—a desert due to low rainfall and ash soil as well as because it is downwind from Kīlauea's fumes and acid rain—gives way to cool misty forests, then bare rocky slopes with

Lava fountains erupting from rift on slopes of Mauna Loa, 1984.

seasonal snow at Mauna Loa's 13,677-foot summit.

Mauna Loa is older and much larger than Kīlauea, and has less of the newer volcano's youthful exuberance. Even before its long-lasting Pu'u 'Ō'ō eruption began, Kīlauea erupted every few years. Mauna Loa's activity seems to be slowing down; for much of re-corded history its eruptions averaged one every four years, though it has now been quiet since 1984. But the 1984 eruption provided us with one of the most memorable sights in our years of volcano watching. Kīlauea was then in an episodic phase, fountaining high columns of lava about once a month. One night as we watched the distant glow of Mauna Loa's new flows Kīlauea burst forth with its own dazzling display. We climbed to the top of an old cinder cone for a better view, and for one night we watched the Hawaiian sky glowing red all around the horizon as our two favorite volcanoes erupted at the same time—a truly unforgettable sight.

Home burning in Kalapana subdivision.

ILLUSTRATION BY DARLECE CLEVELAND

The islands that most people think of as the Hawaiian Chain stretch from the Island of Hawai'i where the oldest rocks are less than a million years old and the youngest are still forming, northwest across the Pacific to Kaua'i where the oldest rocks are 5 million years old. But the chain actually extends far beyond that—past Kaua'i it continues in a northwesterly direction for 2,500 miles with the remnants of eroded, mostly submerged islands of older and older origin.

Scientists long debated the reason for this strange age progression, but in the 1960s a plausible theory emerged. Scientists now believe that the Earth's surface is broken into about a dozen plates that are slowly moving in relation to one another. Most volcanoes are found at the edges, where the plates pull away or override each other. Occasionally, though, there is a "hot spot" beneath the middle of a plate, generating a series of vol-

canoes as the plate moves slowly over it. Hawai'i, in the middle of the Pacific Plate, seems to be over one of these hot spots, which sends a plume of molten rock to the surface. Since the plate is moving over the hot spot at a rate of about four inches a year, the plume—or conduit—eventually gets bent over too far, a new conduit forms, and a new group of volcanoes starts building.

Hawaiian volcanoes are born on the deep ocean floor under 16,500 feet of water. Quiet outpourings of lava go on intermittently, and largely undetected, for thousands of years as the mound builds closer to the surface of the ocean.

When the growing volcano is within a few hundred feet of the surface, gas in the lava and steam from boiling seawater are able to expand rapidly and explosive eruptions start. Rocks and debris are sprayed high in the air, forming a cone of loose ash. Ash is easily washed away by the

sea, but once the cone is above water the eruptions become quieter, with liquid lava flows that gradually armor the growing mountain against the waves and a new island is born.

Even now the newest Hawaiian island is starting to grow. Scientists have detected eruptions of an undersea volcano about 30 miles southeast of the Island of Hawai'i. It has been named Lō'ihi, and should break the surface of the ocean in about ten thousand years.

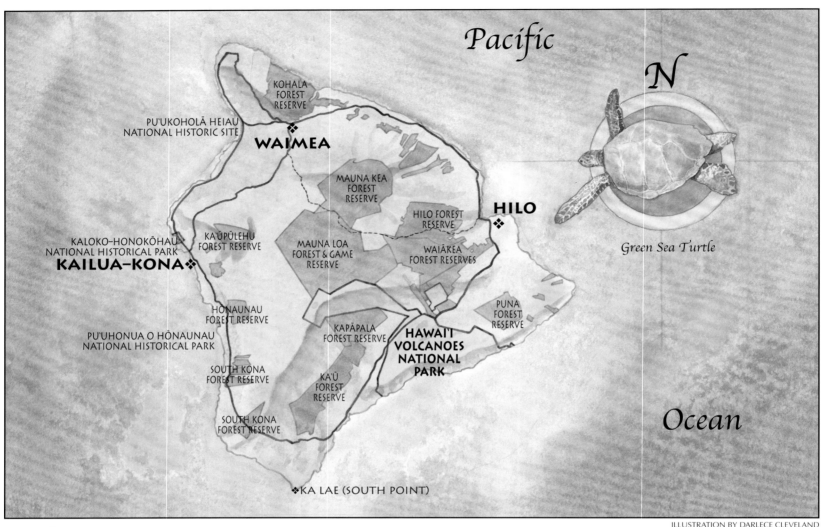

Pacific

N

KOHALA FOREST RESERVE

PU'UKOHOLĀ HEIAU NATIONAL HISTORIC SITE

WAIMEA

MAUNA KEA FOREST RESERVE

HILO FOREST RESERVE

HILO

KALOKO-HONOKŌHAU NATIONAL HISTORICAL PARK

KA'ŪPŪLEHU FOREST RESERVE

MAUNA LOA FOREST & GAME RESERVE

WAIĀKEA FOREST RESERVES

KAILUA-KONA

HŌNAUNAU FOREST RESERVE

PU'UHONUA O HŌNAUNAU NATIONAL HISTORICAL PARK

KAPĀPALA FOREST RESERVE

HAWAI'I VOLCANOES NATIONAL PARK

PUNA FOREST RESERVE

SOUTH KONA FOREST RESERVE

KA'Ū FOREST RESERVE

SOUTH KONA FOREST RESERVE

Green Sea Turtle

Ocean

❖KA LAE (SOUTH POINT)

ILLUSTRATION BY DARLECE CLEVELAND

The Island of Hawai'i, the largest in the Hawaiian Chain, is called the Big Island by people who live there in order to avoid confusion, since the state and island have the same name. At 4,021 square miles, the Island of Hawai'i, built by five great volcanoes, is larger than the rest of the state put together. Since the base of the island's volcanoes lie on sea floor, 16,500 feet beneath the surface, the summits of Mauna Kea and Mauna Loa, both more than 13,500 feet above sea level, can be argued to be even higher mountains than Mount Everest if measured from their base.

The 20° North Latitude line passes through the Island of Hawai'i. This global position defines it as a tropical island within the trade wind zone. However, since temperature decreases with elevation, and rainfall diminishes from windward to leeward, the slopes and shapes of the volcanoes have profound effects on the island's tropical lo-

cation. It is claimed that the Island of Hawai'i has nearly every one of the major climate zones of Earth—from tropical humid at the city of Hilo, a seaport on its windward (northeast) side, to dry arctic conditions at the telescopes on the summit of Mauna Kea. In Hawai'i Volcanoes National Park you can drive or hike around the rim of 2- to 3-mile-wide Kīlauea Caldera through a fern-'ōhi'a rain forest on its windward (northeast) side, and the Ka'ū Desert on its southwest (leeward) side.

In New England there is a saying, "If you don't like the weather, wait ten minutes". On the Island of Hawai'i this could be changed to, "If you don't like the weather, drive ten miles." To a mainland visitor the diversity of the microclimates is astonishing. You could ski on Mauna Kea and snorkel in the warm ocean on the Kona Coast the same day. The small size and rapid change of the microclimates create their own local jargon. On

the Island of Hawai'i real estate agents advertise "dry side" versus "green side" home locations for the leeward versus windward sides of the small town of Waimea.

Besides its size, nearly as large as the state of Connecticut, and its great diversity of climates and vegetation, the landscape of the Island of Hawai'i has one more surprise in store—extensive areas of black, barren lava. In Hawai'i Volcanoes National Park many of these starkly beautiful lava fields are newly created, only a few years old. Like some places in the desert, these areas are barren of vegetation, but not of beauty.

OPPOSITE: Pāhoehoe lava and colonizing kupukupu (common swordfern). PHOTO© BY LARRY ULRICH

Volcano Dynamics

Pu'u 'Ō'ō vent, 1983.   USGS PHOTO BY JOHN DVORAK

The forces of nature in Hawaiian legends belong to Gods and Goddesses, just as they do in the myths of ancient Greece and Rome. The word volcano comes from Vulcan, Roman God of Fire. In Hawai'i, he is a she; Pele, Goddess of Volcanoes and keeper of their fires.

Pele's present home is in Kīlauea Volcano, but one legend says her arrival in Hawai'i began on Ni'ihau, the most northwesterly of the eight main islands. Next she ventured to Kaua'i, and then along the island chain to her present home. This Pele migration legend closely parallels the ages of the islands determined by modern science. The Hawaiians were keen observers of nature; they could see that the landscapes of Kaua'i looked older than those of the Island of Hawai'i.

Modern scientific views on how volcanoes work involve more physics and chemistry than Gods and Goddesses, but plenty of mysteries remain. We know from deep mines and holes drilled into the Earth that temperature increases with depth. This heat comes mainly from the natural radioactive breakdown of uranium, thorium, and rare atoms of potassium. All rocks, including lava, contain very small amounts of these tiny heaters.

So how can these tiny heaters melt rocks? First, rocks are good insulators; they do not conduct heat very well. Second, the heating goes on very slowly, but over long periods of geologic time. Try this thought experiment: If you put enough covers on your bed so that almost no heat escapes from your body, your temperature will slowly build up to levels that could kill you. Before that happens you throw off some blankets. In the Earth, volcanoes vent some of that heat build-up long before the world melts.

A hundred miles below the Earth's surface, temperatures are close to the melting point of common rocks, but volcanoes are not evenly spread over the globe. Many of them, like Mount St. Helens and Mount Fuji, occur where the Earth's plates converge. Others, like Hekla Volcano in Iceland, once thought to be a portal to hell, occur where plates pull apart. But Hawaiian volcanoes occur within the Pacific Plate, thousands of miles from the nearest plate edges. Geologists call them hot-spot volcanoes, although the origin of hot spots is a subject of lively debate.

Once a large blob of rock becomes molten in the depths of the Earth it tends to rise toward the surface. Like in a "lava lamp" the lighter blob of molten rock, called magma, moves upward because it is less dense than the surrounding cooler rocks. Any deep fractures, like those near the plate edges, will assist this rise by acting as conduits. If and when magma reaches the surface, dissolved gases like water and carbon dioxide boil out, and the degassed magma, now called molten lava, pours forth. Eruptions of lava are intermittent if the rate of lava emission exceeds the rate of magma supply from depth. In long-lasting eruptions, like the Pu'u 'Ō'ō eruption of Kīlauea, the eruption rate and the supply rate from depth are in close balance. But many Hawaiian eruptions, like the last one from Mauna Loa that lasted only three weeks, rapidly pour out great volumes of lava and soon exhaust their supply.

Rocks that melt to form magma are part of the Earth's mantle, which is composed of dense minerals like olivine, the gemstone of people born in August. Only the most easily melted part of mantle rock becomes magma, and worldwide that molten fraction is basaltic, a silica melt whose composition is not very different than brown beer-bottle glass. After eruption and cooling, basaltic magma becomes just plain basalt—a dense, hard, black rock that builds volcanoes. Basalt is not the only volcanic rock, but it is the world's most common one. The Hawaiian Islands are 99.9% basalt.

In the Azores, volcanic islands in the Atlantic Ocean, there is an old Portuguese saying that "the rock is the mother of the soil". This same basic idea, even if not so clearly expressed, is understood by all agrarian cultures. Basalt weathers into clay minerals—rapidly in warm areas with high rainfall, and much more slowly in cold, dry climates. Lichen, ferns, and finally trees grow and die on the lava flows, adding compost that speeds the breakdown of the rock into soil. On the rainy areas of Kīlauea, lava flows only decades old begin to support trees, and in a few hundred years the flows are hidden by lush vegetation. In stark contrast, lava flows thousands of years old near the summit of Mauna Loa appear

OPPOSITE: Spatter cone and flow inside Pu'u 'Ō'ō Crater. PHOTO© G. BRAD LEWIS

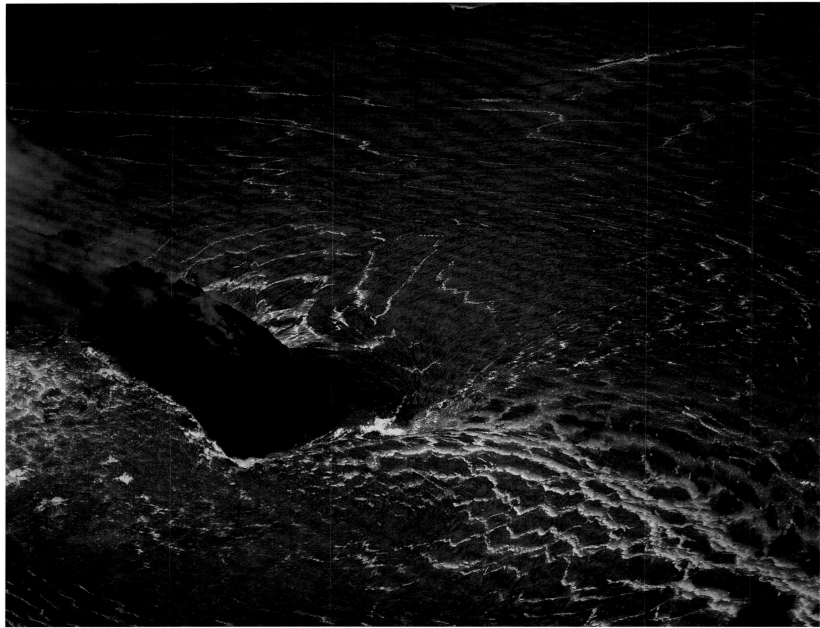

Active lava lake in Pu'u 'Ō'ō Crater.

much the same as they did when they first cooled and hardened.

Most eruptions of Kīlauea and Mauna Loa are not violently explosive. The main reasons for this include the fact that the magma that creates explosive volcanoes contains more dissolved gases and is more viscous. The sticky molten lava tends to be torn into fragments as the trapped gases violently escape. Spectacular lava fountains do occur in Hawai'i as lava spurts from narrow vents, but in general the Hawaiian eruptions are relatively gentle and predictable compared to Pacific Rim volcanoes, and they can be viewed in reasonable safety from proper viewpoints.

Some understanding of how volcanoes work does not diminish their awesome wonder. The complex and beautifully balanced way the Earth works is a wonder in itself.

Lava fountain and cascade, Mauna Ulu, 1969.

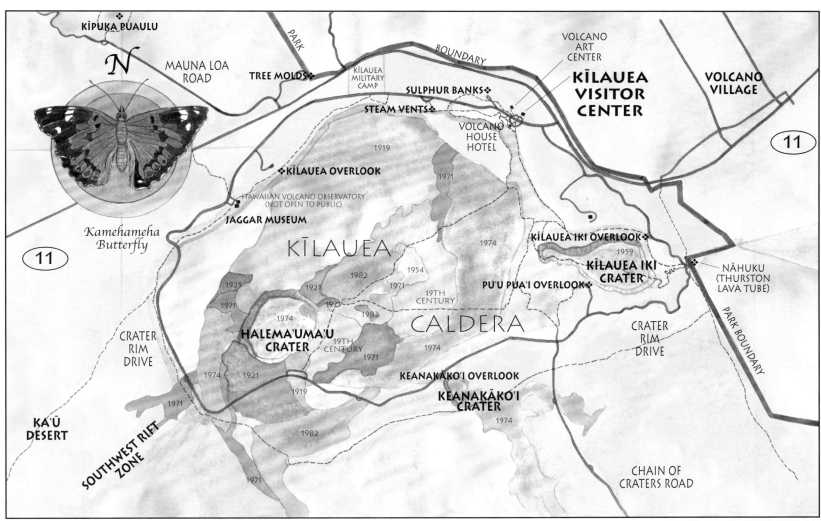

The following labels appear on the map:

KĪPUKA PUAULU

MAUNA LOA ROAD

TREE MOLDS❖

PARK BOUNDARY

VOLCANO ART CENTER

KĪLAUEA VISITOR CENTER

VOLCANO VILLAGE

KĪLAUEA MILITARY CAMP

SULPHUR BANKS❖

STEAM VENTS❖

VOLCANO HOUSE HOTEL

11

1919

❖KĪLAUEA OVERLOOK

1971

HAWAIIAN VOLCANO OBSERVATORY (NOT OPEN TO PUBLIC)

JAGGAR MUSEUM

Kamehameha Butterfly

11

KĪLAUEA

KĪLAUEA IKI OVERLOOK❖

1974

1959

KĪLAUEA IKI CRATER

NĀHUKU (THURSTON LAVA TUBE)

1954

1982

PU'U PUA'I OVERLOOK❖

19TH CENTURY

1921

1921

1971

CALDERA

CRATER RIM DRIVE

PARK BOUNDARY

1971

1974

1982

HALEMA'UMA'U CRATER

19TH CENTURY

1974

CRATER RIM DRIVE

KA'Ū DESERT

1974

1921

1919

KEANAKĀKO'I OVERLOOK

KEANAKĀKO'I CRATER

1971

SOUTHWEST RIFT ZONE

1982

1974

CHAIN OF CRATERS ROAD

1971

ILLUSTRATION BY DARLECE CLEVELAND

The flat, barren floor of Kīlauea Caldera and the 400-foot cliffs that surround it create a strangely beautiful, out-of-this-world panorama. Visitors standing on its rim expecting to see a steep conical mountain often ask, "Where is the volcano?" Geologists call this summit feature of Kīlauea Volcano a caldera rather than a crater because it is very large—three miles long and two miles wide—and was formed mainly by collapse instead of explosion. Nevertheless, early explorers and mapmakers used the word crater, so both names are correct.

Inside the caldera is a smaller crater, Halema'uma'u, 3,000 feet across, and in the year 2001, 280 feet deep. From the caldera rim it appears as a dark circular hole. Halema'uma'u has been the main focus of volcanic activity of Kīlauea for the past two centuries, and is the legendary home of Pele. Volcanic fumes rise from Halema'uma'u as they have for more than a century. As Mark Twain said about Kīlauea, "The smell of sulphur is strong, but not unpleasant to a sinner."

Both Kīlauea Caldera and Halema'uma'u Crater were created by collapse when magma stored beneath them moved to some other location. The last time this happened to the entire caldera was in 1790, and to just Halema'uma'u, in 1924. Both were hundreds of feet deeper just after the collapses occurred; their present flat floors are the result of many flows of lava that have since ponded and cooled within them. The latest eruption inside the caldera occurred in 1982. It was a small flow that covered part of Crater Rim Drive in the south end of the caldera. Within a few weeks the National Park Service had the road reopened even though the bulldozer turned up slabs of the hardened but still hot pāhoehoe.

We recommend the hike across the floor of Kīlauea Caldera on a trail that descends through the forest from Volcano House to the rim of Halema'uma'u Crater. This 3-mile-long trail (one way) across the pāhoehoe and 'a'ā lava flows of 19th and 20th Century eruptions has been compared to walking on the moon. Indeed, hiking across and studying the volcanic features in Kīlauea Caldera was an important part of the field training for the astronauts before their historic trips to the real moon. Arrange for a car to meet you at the Halema'uma'u parking lot, or plan on a five-hour, round-trip hike to Volcano House. A trail guide is available at the Kīlauea Visitor Center. The sulfur fumes at Halema'uma'u may be irritating or harmful to people with breathing problems or heart trouble.

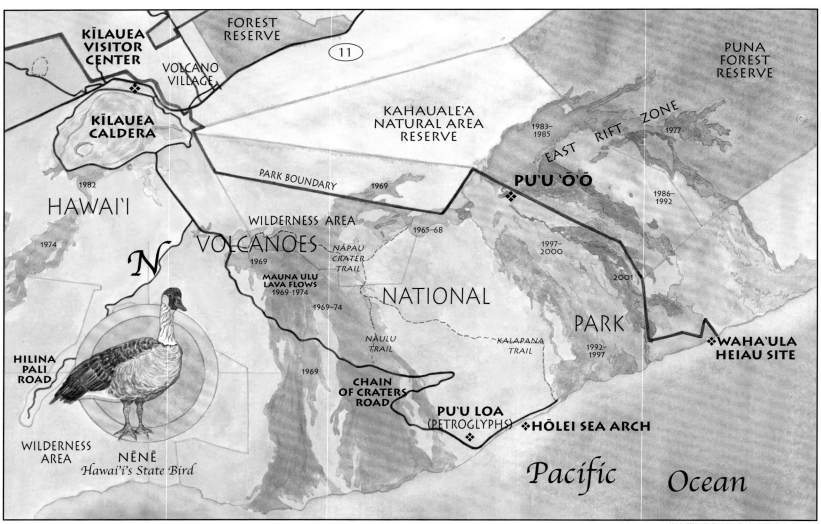

ILLUSTRATION BY DARLECE CLEVELAND

The tremor alarm was triggered just after midnight on January 2, 1983, bringing geologists racing to the Hawaiian Volcano Observatory to check their instruments. They found the seismographs dancing with volcanic tremor and small earthquakes—no false alarm this time. The tremor, a low-frequency ground vibration, suggested that magma was moving at shallow depths, and the small earthquakes showed that rocks were breaking as magma wedged into newly forming cracks. By measuring the small differences in arrival times of the earthquake waves at different seismic stations, the sources of the quakes were soon pinpointed along the east rift of Kīlauea. Pele was on the move again.

Missionary William Ellis, in 1823, was the first non-Hawaiian to visit Kīlauea Caldera, and was told by his guides that it had been burning from "time immemorial". Questioned about eruptions on the volcano's flanks, they answered that there had been many, and that "they supposed Pele went by a road underground from her house in the crater to the shore."

Making a map of that "road underground" is part of the observatory's research program, and this new intrusion of magma breaking open an underground crack was providing important information. Small earthquakes continued throughout the night and next day, and their locations outlined the growing dike—the magma-filled fissure—as a thin, vertical fracture breaking slowly un-derground down the east side of Kīlauea at about one-half-mile per hour. The growing dike was five miles long and two miles from top to bottom. Its top before the eruption began was about two miles below the surface. Earthquake locations do not provide any information on the width of a growing dike, but prehistoric dikes that have been exposed by erosion are usually only a few feet wide. Thousands of these dike intrusions have cracked the sides of Kīlauea during its lifetime, clustered along areas of weakness called rift zones.

But back to the geologists who were plotting the migration of the new magma intrusion along Kīlauea's east rift. The tip of the dike stopped moving down rift about midday on January 2nd, and then more shallow

Finally the crack reached the surface of the rift about 10 miles east of Kīlauea Caldera shortly past midnight on January 3rd. The beginning of the eruption was dramatic with lines of lava fountains spouting "curtains of fire" along a fissure nearly four miles long. This area of the east rift includes dense rainforest and rugged lava fields from previous eruptions with no roads and only poor trails, but geologists were there to witness the breakout.

Back at the observatory, another important instrument—a recording tiltmeter—was providing additional data about the eruption. Magma feeding the eruption was apparently being supplied from a source about three miles beneath the summit of Kīlauea, and the summit region was subsiding. The summit tiltmeter began to show subsidence only an hour after the earthquake swarm heralded the beginning of the intrusion, and continued steadily until the first interruption of lava emission occurred the morning of January 3rd. Used to many previous short-lived eruptions, most volcano watchers at this point thought the eruption was over. Little did they know that this was just the beginning of an east-rift eruption that has continued for 19 years and is still going strong.

Off and on lava fountains along the initial fissures continued until June 1983 when a single vent became the focal point of the eruption. A large cone of lava spatter and cinders, later named Pu'u 'Ō'ō (Hill of the 'Ō'ō bird), built up around this vent. Its intermittent eruptions were spectacular—high, roaring lava fountains spouting as high as 1,500 feet for hours, with fall back of molten lava spatter and hardened lava cinders adding new layers to the growing cone. Forty-four episodes of these giant lava fountains that roared away for about a day occurred roughly once a month. 'A'ā flows from these gushing fountains moved slowly down the southeast side of Kīlauea, and were the first

to destroy homes in Royal Gardens, a remote subdivision just outside the national park.

In July 1986, the vent unexpectedly moved two miles down rift from Pu'u 'Ō'ō and began erupting in an entirely different way. Instead of the brief, high-volume lava fountains followed by weeks of repose while Pele rested, the new vent poured out lava at a slower but more continuous rate. The new vent was named Kūpaianaha ("the mysterious one" in Hawaiian), and geologists referred to this new phase as a steady-state eruption. The high fountains that had cooled the lava and created 'a'ā flows during the previous phase were replaced by hotter pāhoehoe flows that welled from the new vent and slowly but steadily moved down the side of Kīlauea toward the sea. Many of these pāhoehoe flows cooled and crusted over, but their molten interior kept running through lava tubes to feed their growing fronts. Breaks, called skylights, in the roofs of these active lava tubes provided amazing views of red-hot lava rushing through.

It took four months for the flows from Kūpaianaha to reach the ocean. When they did, great plumes of steam arose from the 2,100°F lava trying to boil away the sea. Another Hawaiian legend tells of the fights between Pele and Namakaokaha'i, Goddess of the Sea. These are violent conflicts: Pele may briefly win and extend her lava lands, but Namakaokaha'i is more patient and eventually reclaims them.

Sulfur in the molten lava and chlorine in the ocean water give a hellish touch to the rising steam where lava enters the sea. Their chemistry adds acrid-smelling acid droplets to the rising vapor clouds. Since 1986, when the current eruption reached the ocean, these great steam plumes, visible for miles along the park's southeast coastal road, have provided millions of volcano-watchers a spectacular view. Those hiking closer along a rough "trail" from the lava-covered end of the road to designated viewpoints may ac-

tually see streams of red rock pouring into the sea, but beware. The new land being built into the water is unstable and large areas—as big as a football field—often slide beneath the sea. Sudden steam explosions may also occur when a wave crashes into the open end of a lava tube. Four people who ventured too close have been killed by such hazards so don't go beyond the marked viewpoints. The best viewing is at dusk but the hiking is rough. Here are a few precautions: Take a flashlight (and extra batteries), wear sturdy shoes, and pants that can protect your legs in a fall; the surface of hardened lava is basalt glass, and its broken edges are sharp. Carry plenty of water, and for daytime hikes be sure to use sunscreen.

Lava from Kūpaianaha destroyed the village of Kalapana in 1990. No one was killed or hurt; the flows moved too slowly for that, but about 100 homes were burned and buried by the relentless, creeping advance of molten rock. Lava filled the bay and covered the famous Kaimū black sand beach. Many Hawaiians who lived in Kalapana were remarkably philosophical about their loss. "No one has been hurt", they said, "and after all, it's Pele's land."

In 1992, the vent at Kūpaianaha shut down and the activity moved back to Pu'u 'Ō'ō, but it continued the slow, steady-state style that began in 1986. No more of the great intermittent lava fountains have occurred, and newly formed lava tubes have continued to feed flows into the sea. As of 2001, the Pu'u 'Ō'ō/Kūpaianaha eruption has poured out one-half cubic mile of lava covering 40 square miles. How long will this record breaking eruption continue? That is a question the volcano observatory geologists cannot yet answer. They keep trying, but for now it is still Pele's secret.

PAGE 20/21: Pu'u 'Ō'ō eruption adjacent to newly formed cinder cone, 1986. USGS PHOTO BY J.D. GRIGGS

Mauna Loa (13,677 ft.) seen in background from snow-capped Mauna Kea (13,796 ft.).

PHOTO© MICHAEL T. STEWART

Mauna Loa is Earth's greatest living volcano. Measured from the ocean floor, it is higher than Mount Everest, and its 39 recorded eruptions place it among the world's most active. Its 19,000-cubic-mile volume—enough to cover the entire State of California with nearly 600-feet of lava—makes it by far Earth's largest young volcano. Yet, a clear view of Mauna Loa's smooth and gentle slopes belies its great size. It is a classic shield volcano, appearing like a warrior's shield lying face-up on the ground.

Mauna Loa's latest eruption in 1984 caused great concern in Hilo as lava flows moved toward the city. First signs of its awakening began in 1983 with increasing numbers of small earthquakes. Tremor began about two hours before the eruption started on March 25, but the alarm failed that night, and observatory geologists received a good ribbing from astronomers on Mauna Kea who first reported the glow.

The eruption began with lava fountains in Mauna Loa's caldera as a dike injection split the entire summit area. The vents then moved northeast in spectacular lines of fountains, some as high as 100 feet and more than a mile long, that migrated down rift. As lower vents opened, the higher vents stopped erupting. By evening a fountain at the 9,500-foot-elevation, 12 miles northeast of the original summit outbreak, became the principal source of the eruption. A large lava flow from this final vent moved down the volcano toward Hilo. By March 28, this flow had traveled 15 miles, aimed straight at the city only ten more miles away.

International television and newspaper journalists arrived to witness the destruction. Concern was high and proposals to divert the flow by aerial bombing were seriously considered. The idea is that since long 'a'ā lava flows are fed by a central channel, bombs could break down a levee on the side of the flow channel and lava would spill out and form a new flow. In theory, this would slow down the flow's advance toward Hilo.

Fortunately, a levee on the lava channel eight miles upstream collapsed on its own, diverting the flow into a parallel river of lava. It took the front of this new flow five days to reach the same elevation above Hilo as the original flow, and by this time the volume of the eruption was waning. More channel diversions occurred even farther upstream, and, by April 15, the eruption was over. Hilo was saved; only the out-of-town reporters were disappointed.

OPPOSITE: Cone inside Moku'āweoweo Caldera, Mauna Loa. PHOTO© G. BRAD LEWIS.

EVOLUTION IN HAWAI'I

Kamehameha butterfly.   PHOTO© JACK JEFFREY

Because of its unique island ecology, Hawai'i ranks first in the world for its count of endemic species—those that occur naturally nowhere else on Earth. No place is more geographically isolated; the nearest continental land mass is nearly 2,500 miles away. All life that arrived on the bare volcanic islands after the steaming lava had cooled had to come by swimming in, or floating on, the ocean, by flying or drifting through the air, or by hitchhiking in the feathers or digestive tracts of migrating birds. Hawai'i's only two native mammals are a small brown bat and the Hawaiian monk seal; one came by air and the other by sea.

It is hard to imagine that any living organism could survive the journey and establish itself here, but over millions of years a wide variety of plants, insects, snails, and birds was able to colonize successfully. There were few, if any, competitors, and the varied climate zones and topography of the Hawaiian Islands afforded an astonishing number of ecological niches to fill. The new arrivals evolved and diversified rapidly in unexpected and surprising directions, giving Hawai'i an unequaled native flora and fauna. The isolation of these remote islands set the stage for one of history's most remarkable experiments in evolution.

The absence of large grazing or browsing animals was key to the successful adaptation of the newly arrived plants. They were able to evolve into specialized forms that could survive in bogs, deserts, rainforests, and even alpine conditions, but along the way they lost most of their defense mechanisms: spines, thorns, even strong odors.

Some Hawaiian plants came to exhibit what botanists call arborescence, or a tendency to evolve into woody, tree-like forms— like the species of violet with a strong, woody stem that grows to more than eight feet tall. A spectacular example of arborescence is the group of Hawaiian lobelias—known to home gardeners as small, colorful flowers. Hawai'i has more than 100 species of lobelia, ranging from two to almost 40 feet in height.

Perhaps the most spectacular evolutionary story is that of Hawai'i's birds. Biologists like to say that if Darwin had come to Hawai'i before he saw the Galapagos he would never have left.

Very few land birds—probably 15 species—found their way across vast distances to Hawai'i, but they evolved into more than 70 species. One of the most amazing examples of adaptive radiation is the Hawaiian honeycreeper; these small, brilliantly colored birds are probably descendants of some sort of finch, but they diversified into as many as 50 different species to fill a broad range of ecological niches. Some developed long, curved bills to sip nectar from flowers, some have stout, parrotlike bills to crack big seeds, and others have straight bills for picking insects from crevices.

Safe from predators to worry about, some birds took what turned out to be an unfortunate evolutionary turn and became flightless; many others built their nests in unprotected places on the ground. Other life forms evolved in stranger ways, including an eyeless spider that spends its life deep in dark lava tubes, or the world's only known carnivorous caterpillar, that hides in leaves to ambush its prey.

Several million years of this very slow colonization passed; some say perhaps only one new life form arrived every 10,000 years. But the life-form that arrived about 1600 years ago—*homo sapiens*—had the most profound effect on this isolated ecological system. The Polynesians, and the pigs, dogs, and rats they brought with them, unwittingly began to utterly transform native ecosystems. Flightless birds were easy prey, and some were hunted to extinction. Increasing populations needed more food and housing, and in many areas, much of the native vegetation below 1,500 feet in elevation was cleared for agricultural activities. The arrival of Captain James Cook in 1778, and the explorers who followed him, signaled the beginning of drastic, sometimes irreversible changes to the natural and cultural landscapes of Hawai'i.

The native Hawaiian population lacked immunity and was quickly decimated by newly introduced diseases. Cattle, sheep, goats, and European pigs were set free and soon became wild. They grazed, stomped, and rooted their way through defenseless native ecosystems, causing the extinctions of countless plants,

---

OPPOSITE: Young koa forest near Tree Molds, Mauna Loa Road. PHOTO© JON GNASS

Sea turtle on black sand beach at Punalu'u Beach County Park.

birds, and invertabrates. Hundreds of species of alien plants and animals were being introduced, altering the balance still further.

Beginning in the early 1800s, native forests were cleared for ranching, and vast quantities of the highly prized and fragrant sandalwood tree were lumbered and sent to China. The result of all this was disaster for Hawai'i's native flora and fauna. It has been said that there have been more animal and plant species extinguished in the Hawaiian Islands than in all of North America.

It was not until early in the 20th Century that botanists and biologists began to realize the extent of what was happening and how many treasures were being lost. Once recognized, efforts were made to stem the tide; many conservation groups now work to halt the wave of man-induced extinctions.

Hawai'i Volcanoes National Park has taken a lead in this effort; ambitious fencing and hunting projects are controlling the voracious goat population and the feral pigs that have been so destructive to rainforest vegetation. Identifying and eradicating alien plants like faya tree, kahili ginger, and banana poka gives the native flora the chance to flourish in this special environment, and the native birds and insects are encouraged to return. Because of this effort, Hawai'i Volcanoes National Park has been named an International Biosphere Reserve.

Mongoose, a species introduced to Hawai'i.

OPPOSITE: Hōlei Sea Arch near the end of Chain of Craters Road, dusk.

The nēnē bears a striking resemblance to the Canada goose.

PHOTO© G. BRAD LEWIS

NĒNĒ—HAWAI'I'S STATE BIRD

The Hawaiian goose, or nēnē, is thought to have evolved from the same ancestral stock as the water-loving Canada goose, but in Hawai'i it has adapted to a much different environment. Here they spent more time walking over rough lava flows than swimming in lakes, and as a consequence lost much of the characteristic webbing on their feet. Except for that difference, they closely resemble their ancestor—gray and brown with black markings and about 20 inches tall.

Experts believe that as many as eight other species of geese may have evolved from the same ancestors, but almost all of those were flightless. All but the nēnē are extinct, probably because the nēnē are excellent flyers (though they seem to prefer to walk).

But the nēnē too came close to extinction. Even though they could fly they made their nests on the ground and so were easy prey for predators—both animal and human. Introduced cats, dogs, and mongooses took a heavy toll, and many were hunted for food. Though they numbered in the tens of thousands at the time of European contact in the late 18th century, by the 1950s there were only 33 known in existence, and half of those were in captivity.

Ambitious programs for captive breeding and release were started in the 1970s by the National Park Service, the State of Hawai'i, and the Wildfowl Trust in England. By now their numbers have increased to the point that in Hawai'i Volcanoes and Haleakalā National Parks some have been released into the wild. No one knows whether they will eventually be able to survive and reproduce in a natural state; all their old enemies are still around, and while they are no longer hunted they have another formidable hazard—the automobile. Nēnē are apt to wander into parking lots or across busy roads, and many have been killed or injured by cars. Please don't contribute to this problem by feeding the nēnē.

Efforts by park biologists to improve their chances of survival include trying to control predators, especially in nesting areas. They even provide some predator-free enclosures where the birds can rest in safety. Time will tell whether or not the nēnē population can survive and thrive without help—their many admirers hope so. Hawaiian residents have named the handsome nēnē their State Bird.

OPPOSITE: Opening in roof of lava tube, Kīlauea, 1997. PHOTO© G. BRAD LEWIS

1995 pāhoehoe lava flow near Chain of Craters Road.

THE LAND RECOVERS

At first glance a new lava field looks like permanent desolation. How could life possibly reestablish itself on this wasteland of still-cooling solid rock? But it does, of course; all the plant life that arrived when the Hawaiian Islands were forming were met by conditions like these, but some survived and flourished.

Plants re-colonizing on today's lava flows, though, have an easier time of it than did their ancestors because seeds and spores don't have to travel from faraway islands and continents.

For many years biologists have been studying the sequence of plant regrowth after volcanic eruptions and have found that it depends both on colonizers and survivors. Sometimes a major eruption showers a thick blanket of pumice over a large area of vegetation. If the pumice deposit is not too hot a surprising number of trees and shrubs may be able to survive. A large 'ōhi'a tree can withstand a pumice layer almost ten feet thick, and some shrubs and herbs live after being almost totally buried.

But under a solid lava flow there are no survivors. The speed of colonization on these surfaces is controlled largely by the amount of rainfall, but the sequence is roughly the same. Biologists have found that algae always arrive first, followed by lichen, ferns, and mosses. Native woody seed plants appear next, and alien plant species usually come last.

In areas of high rainfall the process starts remarkably soon, and flows only 30 years old may support some native ferns, shrubs, and trees, while on the dry side of the islands flows that are much older look as if they had just been erupted. The lava texture makes a difference too; the rough surface of an 'a'ā flow can catch and hold moisture and seeds more efficiently than can a slick pāhoehoe flow. But on a pāhoehoe flow a crack can trap some moisture, and it is a special pleasure to see a tiny fern sprouting from such an inhospitable surface.

A lava flow may follow a somewhat capricious path downhill, and sometimes will move around an area of land leaving it isolated but not covering it. The Hawaiian word for such a place is kīpuka. Almost islands in themselves, kīpuka often have deep, fertile soils and play a very important role in providing seed sources for re-colonizing the adjacent sterile flows.

OPPOSITE: Rainforest on Kīlauea near Nāhuku (Thurston Lava Tube). PHOTO© BRUCE JACKSON/GNASS PHOTO IMAGES

History Begins

Members of the Royal Court in their colorful, flowing capes. PHOTO© MICHAEL T. STEWART

The geologic history of Hawai'i may have begun millions of years ago, but human history began only about 1,600 years ago when a voyaging canoe from the Marquesas made landfall on one of the Hawaiian Islands. It was an epic voyage, with one or more large double-hulled canoes, each capable of carrying about 20 people plus provisions to keep them alive on a 2,400-mile journey. They were intrepid explorers but more than that, they were intent on settling a new land and had come prepared to stay. The group included families who brought with them materials they would need to start a new life. The canoes had been fashioned with tools of stone, bone, and coral, with hulls that had been dug out of tree trunks with stone adzes. Great triangular sails were woven from pandanus leaves, and seams were sealed with sap from breadfruit or other tropical trees. Scientists believe they brought more than two dozen different plants, seeds, and cuttings—not just for food but for shelter and medicines. They also bought pigs, dogs, and chicken-like fowl. Nothing in oral tradition suggests why they left the Marquesas—perhaps it was overpopulation, famine, or political disputes—but the Polynesians had always been seafaring people and it may have just been the lure of finding and colonizing a new land.

They had traditional knowledge of celestial navigation; they could read the positions of stars, moon, sun, and wind, and they could also read the signs of the sea—waves, currents, fish, and flotsam. No one knows whether any of Hawai'i's volcanoes were erupting as the voyagers approached the islands, but if one were it would have been like a beacon, visible for more than 100 miles, and seen as a sign from the Gods.

The land they found in Hawai'i must have looked somewhat familiar, with trees, ferns, and herbaceous plants from America and Asia as well as plants that over centuries had evolved from those found on other tropical Pacific Islands. Among the settlers were excellent fishermen and skilled farmers so the transition—while not easy—probably proceeded much as planned.

Amazing as the story of the journey to Hawai'i is, it is even more remarkable that some of the voyagers and navigators sailed back to their Marquesan home, probably to pick up more supplies and new colonists to take back to Hawai'i. Such travel between the islands continued for hundreds of years. The motives for these trips probably included looking for husbands or wives or for skilled craftsmen whose talents were needed, or adding to their supply of materials and plants. Some probably wanted to be buried in their homeland and some may have just been homesick. Whatever the reasons, it is incredible to think that such a voyage could be successfully repeated many times.

After a few hundred years the trips to the Marquesas seem to have stopped. By then the colonists—born in Hawai'i—must have considered it their home and were developing their own culture and customs. Settlements had been built, mostly in the coastal lowlands, where both fishing and agriculture were thriving.

About 1200 AD a new wave of migration took place, probably from Tahiti. These new invaders brought their own customs and Gods to strengthen or replace those they found. Kahuna (priests) proclaimed new kapu (taboos) and started building new heiau (temples). One of the first built in this period was Waha'ula Heiau (the temple of the red mouthed God) on the shoreline, where human sacrifices were performed. The remains of Waha'ula stood until 1997, when it was engulfed and overrun by flows from the Pu'u 'Ō'ō eruption.

Over the next centuries the society that developed was complex and highly stratified. The ali'i (chiefs) were the rulers, with the ali'i nui, the high chief, ruling the whole island. The kahuna were priests or highly skilled specialists, and the maka'āinana were the commoners who did the work, paid the taxes, and observed the rules and kapu that were handed down to them.

The land was divided into moku, or districts, and each was ruled by a chief of lesser rank than the high chief. In an ingenious and practical scheme, each district was divided into wedge-shaped parcels—wide at the coast and tapering to a point in the mountains. These were called ahupua'a, and gave the people living in each one access to the sea, agricultural land, and high forests for building materials and medicinal plants.

Traditional Hawaiian handcarved koa outrigger canoe.

Their religion included four major Gods and countless demigods, as well as the belief that Gods were represented in all forms of nature. Among the demigods was Pele, Goddess of Volcanoes, whose home was Kīlauea Volcano. She was revered, respected, and feared, as Hawaiians recognized her power and the volcanic origin of all the land they occupied.

The arrival of Captain Cook, in 1778, began an era of incredible change for the people and for the land. Explorers, missionaries, and merchants who followed brought a world of new objects, ideas, customs, and religions—and new diseases. Hawaiians soon found their world drastically reshaped. In the century that followed, Hawaiian culture and customs were almost completely submerged by the new "civilization". Fortunately they were not completely lost; in the last two decades there has been a groundswell of interest in—and respect for—Hawaiian language, culture, and oral traditions. There has even been a grandly successful revival of ancient navigational skills—a tribute to those intrepid voyagers who sailed the Polynesian Triangle.

Pu'ukoholā Heiau National Historic Site.

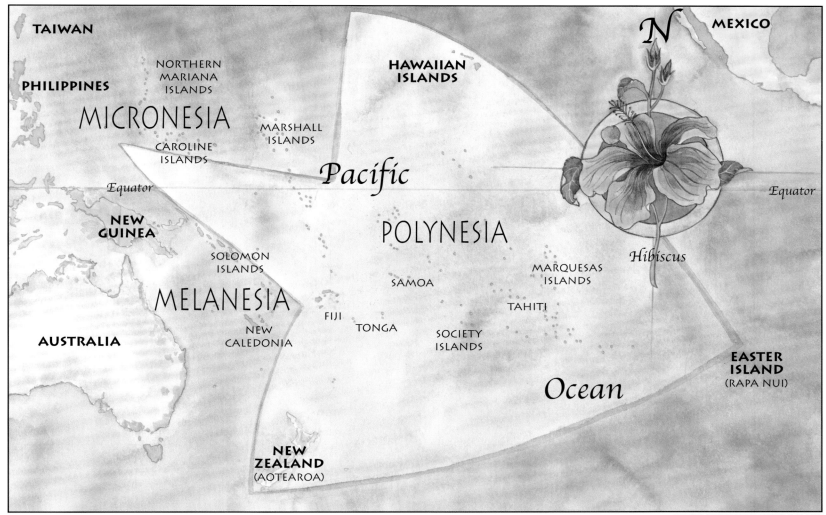

ILLUSTRATION BY DARLECE CLEVELAND

Polynesians explored the Pacific Ocean, nearly half the surface of our planet, long before Vikings crossed the Atlantic. Only the lack of a written history has denied the Polynesians their place, perhaps first place, among the world's other great voyagers like Eriksson, Columbus, and Cook.

The Polynesian Triangle is enormous. From Hawai'i on the north, to New Zealand on the southwest, to Easter Island on the southeast, it covers the Central Pacific. Each side is about 5,000 miles long, the distance between New York and Moscow. By the quality of their double-hulled canoes, their mastery of celestial navigation, and their sheer daring, the Polynesians explored and colonized this vast region of sea and sky.

Even without a written history, chants and stories remembered through many generations, and radiocarbon dating of hundreds of archeological sites, have established a rough timetable of Polynesian colonization. Nowhere else on Earth does only one native language cover so large an area, but slight variations in the sounds and use of words have helped scholars determine the sequence of island group discovery. About 1400 BC people from New Guinea migrated to Samoa and Tonga, and it was there the Polynesian culture developed. Around 300 BC eastward voyages of exploration discovered and settled the Cook Islands, Tahiti, and the Marquesas. By 300 AD voyagers had found and settled Rapa Nui (Easter Island), and by 400 AD, Hawai'i. Finally, Polynesians reached Aotearoa (New Zealand) about 1000 AD. It was not until 1642 that Europeans rediscovered New Zealand.

This amazing discovery and colonization of the Pacific began before the Golden Age of Greece and was completed while Europe struggled through the Dark Ages. It is one of the magnificent feats of human history. These great voyages to small islands across thousands of miles of empty ocean demanded navigational skills that some scholars of Polynesian history thought impossible; they considered the discoveries to be accidental. However, recent voyages from Hawai'i to Tahiti and Rapa Nui in double-hulled canoes using traditional Polynesian navigation have demonstrated that the original discoveries were likely planned and executed with great skill.

Navigation by the direction of sunrise and sunset, and the position of stars, was pioneered by ancient Polynesians. Mary Kawena Pukui, in her book *Hawaiian Proverbs and Poetical Sayings*, includes this one about voyaging: "O na hōkū no na kiu o ka lani—The stars are the spies of Heaven." Someday the world, as well as the stars, will recognize the great contributions Polynesians made to the history of discovery.

TRACINGS OF THE PAST

Early Hawaiians were prolific picture makers; concentrations of rock carvings called petroglyphs are found on all the Hawaiian Islands. Pu'u Loa in Hawai'i Volcanoes National Park holds the largest concentration of these ancient pictures in the islands, with more than 24,000 carvings. It is especially significant because it is the only site in Hawai'i for which a specific function is known. In interviews by anthropologist Martha Beckwith in 1914, local villagers told of its special magic.

Pu'u Loa is a large field of billowing pāhoehoe, about a mile inland from the ocean. The main feature is a long, low hill of lava. "Long Hill" is the literal translation of Pu'u Loa, but Hawaiians interpret it to mean "Hill of Long Life". The top of this central hill is completely covered with at least 7,000 cup-like depressions that were pecked into the lava and appear to be very old. On the flat lava that surrounds the hill in all directions is an incredible array of carvings, almost all incorporating these holes in different designs. Some are simple groups enclosed in a circle, some are holes interconnected in imaginative ways to form designs, and many are human figures associated with groups of holes.

Apparently it was the custom of early Hawaiians to bring to Pu'u Loa the umbilical stump (which they called the piko) of a newborn baby, carve a hole in the rock, put the piko in and cover it with a stone. If the piko was still there in the morning, the child was assured of a long life. This was not just a local custom; families from O'ahu, Maui and even Kaua'i would save the piko of all their children and eventually make the long trip to Pu'u Loa. There they would make a hole for each piko and surround them with a circle to signify a family. Some circles contain as many as 30 or 40 holes. This custom seems to have continued for many generations, well into the late 1800s when it was discouraged by the missionaries.

Besides the "family groups" there are many other pictures and symbols here. In some places the images are carved so close together they overlap, while nearby rocks that look exactly the same have no carvings at all.

Primitive art holds a fascination; for those of us who are not archaeologists, art gives us our clearest glimpse of what was important to the people before the written record. Petroglyphs supply an added dimension because of the permanence of their locations—those we see today are in the same physical setting where they were created. When you walk through a silent petroglyph field today and run your hand over one of the ancient carvings, the sun on your shoulders, the light sea-breeze, and the texture of the rock under your hand all feel the same today as they did to the Hawaiian who carved the image 100 or 1000 years ago.

But if it is easy to re-create the physical environment of the early Hawaiians, the same does not hold true for the mental and emotional environments; those are impossible to duplicate. In the world of the ancient Hawaiian the supernatural was as real as the natural. The images we see reflect a view of the world so different from our own that our intuitions cannot tell us what their symbols may have meant to them. A simple stick figure may symbolize the most solemn appeal to a deity, while a symbol that seems charged with mystery may be just a way of tallying the yam harvest. This is the real problem in interpreting the petrogyphs we see today. We can recognize and admire the graceful figures of men and women, canoes with billowing sails, animals or fish, but we can never be sure why an early Hawaiian was motivated to spend hours in the hot sun, meticulously carving them into the lava.

Petroglyphs at Pu'u Loa.

PHOTO © LAURENCE PARENT

THE VOLCANO WATCHERS

Everyone who ever witnessed a Kīlauea eruption became a volcano watcher—kahuna (Hawaiian priests and priestesses), missionaries, whalers, world travelers, and scientists. Kīlauea continues erupting in 2002, and its present 1.5 million visitors per year also become volcano watchers. Great changes have occurred since missionary William Ellis first wrote about the volcano in 1823. At that time the caldera was more than twice as deep as it is now. Since then, lava lakes and intermittent flows have filled it to its present level. One thing is certain; future volcano watchers will continue to see dramatic changes in the activity and landscape of Kīlauea and Mauna Loa.

Nineteenth Century visitors often penned their impressions of Kīlauea in the guest book of the Volcano House, a primitive lodge on the caldera rim. Mark Twain was apparently not there on a good viewing day, but he did note: "We visited the crater intending to stay all night, but the bottle containing our provisions got broke, and we were obliged to return…7 June 1866." Other visitors were more fortunate. On July 26, 1868, W.D. Alexander wrote: "… nearly the whole of the pit in the southwest end of the crater is in a state of fusion. The display of fireworks tonight was magnificent and shows increasing activity." Isabella Bird, a British writer, entered a long description, but her first line is most impressive. "Arrived yesterday from Hilo after a [horseback] ride of eleven and a half hours. 31 January 1873." Actually the many entries and observations have helped scientists piece together Kīlauea's activity before the Hawaiian Volcano Observatory (HVO) was established.

Thomas Jaggar, a geology professor from MIT, established HVO on the rim of Kīlauea Caldera in 1912, and continued as its director until 1940. The objective of HVO is the scientific study of volcanoes to understand how they work, and to reduce volcanic risk. Financial support for the observatory from universities, Hawaiian businesses, and various government agencies varied over the years and since 1947, HVO has been part of the U.S. Geological Survey.

Jaggar began the careful monitoring of Kīlauea's and Mauna Loa's activity. History often repeats itself on volcanoes, and a good historical record is essential for interpreting what Mother Nature may be up to. Besides recording the visible surface activity of the volcanoes, Jaggar installed seismographs to detect and locate the earthquakes that often precede and accompany eruptions. The pattern, depth, and sequence of these thousands of tiny earthquakes, most too small to be felt, give important clues to what is happening beneath a volcano's surface. Seismic instruments with electronic amplifiers were installed by HVO in the 1950s, and computers to locate the earthquakes quickly, were developed in the 1980s and 90s.

Volcano science is somewhat akin to medicine; the doctor wants to know not only the surface symptoms, but also what is going on inside the patient. The medical analogy can be carried even farther—a live volcano slowly breathes, in the sense that it swells as magma accumulates beneath, and deflates as lava is poured out on its surface. The changing composition and temperature of gases emitted from surface vents are akin to blood tests; they can signal internal changes in magma composition before any surface symptoms may appear.

The inflation and deflation of the ground surface in the summit areas of Kīlauea and Mauna Loa are invisible to the eye, but careful surveying with highly sensitive instruments can detect these changes. One simple method is called optical leveling that involves cementing bench marks in bedrock and leapfrogging with a surveyor's level and tall level rod from one bench mark to the next. By going all the way to sea level, repeated surveys done years apart have shown that the summit of Kīlauea has moved up and down by several feet. It takes a three-person team weeks to level between Hilo and HVO, so other less expensive methods have been established to fill in the relative ups and downs of the summit between the more absolute level surveys.

Electronic tilt meters can detect changes in tilt as small as one part per million—that's the equivalent of putting a dime under one end of a giant carpenter's level 3,000 feet long. Outward tilt measured on the caldera rim indicates the volcano is inflating, while inward tilt indicates deflation. During the high lava-fountain eruptions of Pu'u 'Ō'ō, the summit of Kīlauea tilted inward as magma moved from beneath its summit to supply lava to the vent 12 miles down rift. When the fountaining stopped the summit would slowly re-inflate for about a month until the eruption began again. This cycle repeated some 40 times.

Satellite positioning systems and radar are among the latest high tech methods now being used to detect the pattern of the slow and sometimes erratic "breathing" of these great live volcanoes. Chemical analysis has become sophisticated as well. Gases escaping from surface vents provide checks on the volcanoes' inner workings. Carbon dioxide, sulfur dioxide, and chlorine are given off from magma as it moves upward into regions of lower pressure, but the rate of their release varies among these gases. Studying changes in their ratios helps in understanding whether new batches of magma from much deeper underground are being added to that already stored beneath the volcanoes.

Good old-fashioned field geology also keeps adding new understanding about the prehistoric activity of Kīlauea and Mauna Loa. By mapping the deposits from their ancient eruptions the track record of these volcanoes can be extended back for thousands of years. One recent conclusion from this work is that explosive eruptions in Kīlauea's past were larger and more common

Lava exploding as it pours into the Pacific Ocean.

than previously thought. There is an old saying in geology—"What did happen, can happen." Many catastrophic events are so rare that their recurrence should not be of overwhelming concern to any one person. Institutions, however, responsible for the lives and welfare of thousands or millions of people, need to consider these risks seriously.

Accurately forecasting the timing, location, style, and size of volcanic eruptions is a major but still elusive goal in volcanology. HVO and other volcano observatories around the world have made great progress toward this objective during the 20th Century, and the recent success in predicting the great eruption of Pinatubo Volcano in the Philippines in 1991, suggests that these efforts are

paying off. Besides the scientific progress at HVO, the cooperation between the National Park Service and the U.S. Geological Survey in Hawai'i Volcanoes National Park is a good example of how different government agencies can work together in beneficial ways.

Jaggar at HVO and Lorrin A.Thurston, a Honolulu businessman who strongly supported HVO in its early years, lobbied hard for the creation of a Hawai'i National Park. They argued the ongoing volcanic activity of Kīlauea made it one of the wonders of the globe, and that the list of famous world travelers in the Volcano House guest book was proof of their claim. Congress and the President agreed, and in 1916 they made it official. In 1961 the name was changed to

Hawai'i Volcanoes National Park. The park repaid Jaggar's helping hand in 1987, by building a volcano museum named in his honor adjoining the HVO laboratories. Today, scientists from HVO help the park with its interpretative programs, as well as providing up-to-date information on current volcanic conditions.

Volcano watching can be many things—from a sightseeing drive on a beautiful day in the park to a strenuous adventure hiking up Mauna Loa. It can also be the serious science of trying to understand volcanic processes and reducing the dangers of volcanic eruptions. We were privileged during the years we lived in Hawai'i Volcanoes National Park—we did all these things.

Downed 'ōhi'a along Devastation Trail.
PHOTO© JEFF D. NICHOLAS

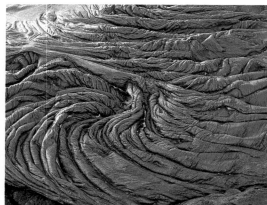
Glowing pāhoehoe flow.
PHOTO© G. BRAD LEWIS

Pāhoehoe river snakes by kīpuka of 40-foot tall 'ōhi'a.
PHOTO© MICHAEL T. STEWART

In Hawai'i Volcanoes National Park, elevations range from sea level to more than 13,000 feet and, as a result, microclimates range from tropical through temperate to alpine. Add to this the complication of variable rainfall controlled by the trade winds—wet on windward mountain slopes, and dry on their lee. This combination of greatly varying temperature and moisture creates an astonishing number of small microclimates. Mark Twain summed it up in one short phrase, "...all the climates of the world in a single glance of the eye."

Biologists recognize ten vegetation zones on the Island of Hawai'i, nine of which occur in the park. They range from coastal lowlands with mainly grasses, through rain forests, to barren stone deserts above 10,000 feet. Even at an in-between elevation like the Crater Rim Drive that circles Kīlauea Caldera at 4,000 feet, climate and vegetation change dramatically in just a few miles. On the northeast rim of the caldera where annual rainfall is close to 100 inches, the road winds through a fern-'ōhi'a rain forest. Only three miles farther on, clockwise, the rapidly thinning forest gives way to the Ka'ū Desert, where annual rainfall is less than 50 inches. Part of the desolation of the Ka'ū is caused by the acid fumes which blow downwind from Halema'uma'u Crater.

Below 1,000 feet, near the Pu'u Loa petroglyph area, bare lava and clumps of dry grasses typify this tropical semi-desert. At higher elevations and rainfall, trees with red blossoms, the 'ōhi'a lehua, begin to appear. The 'ōhi'a, native to Hawai'i, grows over a remarkable range of elevations—from near sea level to 8,000 feet. The rain forest on the windward side of Kīlauea Caldera is a mix of 'ōhi'a trees and huge tree ferns called hāpu'u. The short trail to and from Nāhuku (the Thurston Lava Tube) is a delightful place to walk through this forest and listen to the birds. It's probably no surprise that you may get rained on in a rain forest, but don't worry about snakes. There aren't any in the Park.

Visitors who enjoy overnight backpacking can hike through the dry, lower-elevation zones along the trails to the Park's coastal shelters at Ka'aha, Halapē, or Keauhou. A grove of coconut trees at Halapē was killed when the coast sank below sea level in a major earthquake in 1975. At the other extreme, the hardy few who climb the long trail up Mauna Loa will pass tree line at about 8,500 feet. Above there it is nearly a "no life" zone. Geology students will revel in this land of lava flows, and the more biologically minded can search for the few dwarf plants that survive in this alpine stone desert. Backcountry camping anywhere in the Park is by permit only; register at the Kīlauea Visitor Center before departure.

Coconut palms and grasslands near the coast.
PHOTO© LAURENCE PARENT

Hāpu'u (tree ferns) and 'ōhi'a lehua.
PHOTO© LARRY ULRICH

Rainbow over Ka'ū Desert.
PHOTO© MICHAEL T. STEWART

'Io, Hawaiian hawk.   PHOTO© JACK JEFFREY

'I'iwi.   PHOTO© JACK JEFFREY

Pueo, Hawaiian owl.   PHOTO© JACK JEFFREY

The story of Hawai'i's birds is a complicated one, and scientists are still uncovering lost pieces of the puzzle. It has long been known that a relatively few successful colonizers over several million years evolved into many different species in this splendid island isolation. By a process scientists call adaptive radiation, they managed to fill an astonishing number of evolutionary niches.

The most intriguing story is that of the Hawaiian honeycreepers. From one or maybe two arrivals of small, finch-like birds, as many as 50 species evolved, each filling a different role. Some have stout bills to crush seeds, some bills are curved to sip nectar, some shaped to probe for grubs, and so on. The nectar-sippers are especially interesting; one seems to have evolved side by side with a lobelia whose blossom perfectly echoes the curved bill of the honeycreeper. Most are brilliantly colored; the palila is bright yellow, matching the blooms of the māmane tree on whose seeds it feeds, while the 'apapane is a fluffy red bird that looks like the 'ōhi'a lehua bloom whose nectar it sips.

There are other native birds here; the Hawaiian hawk, or 'io, native to the Island of Hawai'i, the small owl called pueo that prefers daylight hunting, and the 'ōma'o, or Hawaiian thrush, to name a few.

But the downside of the evolutionary story is the staggering number of extinctions. Paleontologists studying bone fragments from extinct birds estimate that between the arrival of the Polynesians more than 1600 years ago and the coming of Captain Cook in 1778, more than 60 bird species became extinct, and by mid-20th Century more than two thirds were gone.

Polynesians—and the dogs, pigs, and rats they brought with them—were extremely destructive to ground-nesting birds. Burning and clearing of lowland forests destroyed the habitat of many of the small forest birds.

When European settlers arrived in Hawai'i they noticed that they saw few birds, so they encouraged the importation of more species—the cardinals, thrushes, bulbuls, the ubiquitous mynahs and others not only crowded out many of the remaining natives but brought with them bird diseases that nearly finished the job. Scientists believe that mosquito-borne avian malaria was a major factor in the decline of native birds throughout the lower elevations. Mosquitoes are thought to have been introduced to the islands as early as 1826, possibly in the water kegs of whaling ships.

Hawai'i Volcanoes National Park provides a safe haven for Hawai'i's remaining threatened bird life. One of the best chances to see (or at least hear) the forest birds is along the trail to Nāhuku (Thurston Lava Tube) on Kīlauea's caldera rim, or in Kīpuka Puaulu.

'Apapane.   PHOTO© JACK JEFFREY

Palila.   PHOTO© JACK JEFFREY

'Akiapōlā'au.   PHOTO© JACK JEFFREY

Uluhe fern. PHOTO© JACK JEFFREY

'Amakihi on māmane tree. PHOTO© JACK JEFFREY

'Ōhelo berries. PHOTO© JEFF D. NICHOLAS

Most of the colorful ornamental plants and flowering trees so abundant in Hawai'i's resorts and towns are imports from other parts of the world but thrive in Hawai'i's felicitous climate. The fragrant plumeria, or frangipani, the flamboyant poinciana, bright orange birds of paradise, bougainvillia, and almost all orchids were brought here but now seem part of the natural scene. Among the few native plants with large colorful flowers are a number of species of hibiscus, most notably a beautiful yellow hibiscus that is the State's official flower.

The native vegetation that clothed these islands before humans arrived had evolved to be highly distinctive, but is now best seen in remote forests or in areas like Hawai'i Volcanoes National Park where native trees and plants are protected from feral animals and alien plant invaders. A walk through Kīpuka Puaulu (Bird Park) or the trail to Nāhuku (Thurston Lava Tube) is like a glimpse of

another world. For exploring the park, a valuable resource is *Trailside Plants of Hawai'i's National Parks* by Charles Lamoureux, available at the Park Visitor Center.

The two most prominent native trees are the 'ōhi'a lehua and the koa. The 'ōhi'a lehua grows in many forms, from small, stunted bushes on new lava flows to tall trees with twisted branches and rounded foliage, towering over tree ferns in the rainforest. Its fluffy red blooms—the lehua—are visited by 'apapane and 'i'iwi, small red honeycreepers that are colored like the flowers.

The majestic koa are the largest trees in the park. They can grow to 100 feet tall and 5 feet in diameter. The beautiful koa wood is highly prized, first by Hawaiians who used the huge logs for canoes and more recently by furniture makers and woodworkers. There are really no large koa forests left,

but some big trees can still be seen in Kīpuka Puaulu and in kīpuka along the Mauna Loa strip road; nice stands of young koa are growing near Park Headquarters and Kīlauea Military Camp.

Sandalwood is another handsome native tree that was logged excessively in the 19th Century when traders realized they could make their fortunes by taking sandalwood to China and trading it for the silks so coveted in Europe and America. Sandalwood forests are gone, but remaining trees are now protected in Hawai'i Volcanoes National Park and Haleakalā National Park. Other native trees to look for are the māmane with bright yellow blossoms, the manele, and, near the coast, the lama—a Hawaiian ebony.

The tree most people associate with the Islands is of course the palm, and with good reason. More than 500 species have been introduced in Hawai'i, and there are at least 30 native loulu palms of the *Pritchardia* genus.

'Ākala berries. PHOTO© JACK JEFFREY

Mauna Kea silversword. PHOTO© JACK JEFFREY

'Āma'u fern. PHOTO© LAURENCE PARENT

Rainforest of hāpu'u and 'ōhi'a lehua.   © JEFF NICHOLAS

Flower of the 'ōhi'a lehua.   PHOTO© JEFF D. NICHOLAS

Morning glory.   PHOTO© JEFF D. NICHOLAS

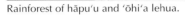

Except for a few right at the coast, however, you probably won't see any in Hawai'i Volcanoes National Park.

Tree ferns, or hāpu'u, make up the dense understory of the rainforests and give them the distinctive Hawaiian appearance. These are huge ferns—sometimes as tall as 30 feet—with shaggy trunks and arching fronds. Smaller native ferns include the swordfern, the uluhe, or false staghorn fern, that grows in nearly-impenetrable thickets, and the 'ama'u, whose new fronds are bright red.

There are several native berries—easiest to see are the 'ōhelo, a small bush with red berries that look like huckleberries, thought by Hawaiians to be sacred to Pele. 'Ōhelo berries are a favorite food of nēnē and the 'ōma'o, or Hawaiian thrush. Other berries are the pūkiawe, with stiff foliage and tiny bright red, pink, or white berries (ornamental, not for eating), and 'ākala, the thornless Hawaiian raspberry.

Another category of plants are those that might have been brought in by Polynesians but also could have arrived by floating seeds; for instance the milo tree, the hau, and the hala; all grow in lowlands near the ocean and have seeds that could survive long distances in the water. Near the coast the beach naupaka, with its strange bloom that looks like a half-flower, and the pōhuehue, or beach morning glory, probably arrived in the same way.

In still another category are those plants brought by the first Polynesians to reach Hawai'i from the South Pacific. With them in their canoes they brought seeds and cuttings of plants they would need to survive in an unknown land. These included food plants like yams, taro for making poi, breadfruit, noni, bananas, and coconuts. Coconut and banana trees were important not only for their fruit but they provided fiber, cording, thatching for roofs, and many other

uses. Ti plants provided wide leaves for wrapping food, other parts for medicinal uses, and even roots that could be boiled and fermented into a sort of beer. They also brought the kukui or candlenut tree; its nuts had several medicinal uses, but also are so oily that a stick with several kukui nuts impaled on it could be lighted for an instant "candle". The kukui bark and leaves were used in tanning, and their dyes were favored for tattooing. Kukui adapted so successfully to the Hawaiian environment that its pale green leaves are seen on hillsides all over the islands, and has been named Hawai'i's State Tree.

Wiliwili tree.   PHOTO© JACK JEFFREY

Pilo berries.   PHOTO© JACK JEFFREY

Koa tree.   PHOTO© G. BRAD LEWIS

Statues at Puʻuhonua o Hōnaunau National Historical Park (Place of Refuge).

HISTORICAL PARKS ON THE ISLAND OF HAWAIʻI

The National Park Service maintains three parks on the west side of Hawaiʻi that provide visitors with a real sense of the way things were on this beautiful island before 1800. The massive stone structures are the most imposing remains, but ghosts of the creative and complex Hawaiian culture—isolated from the rest of the world for more than 1400 years—pervade these historic places.

Puʻuhonua o Hōnaunau National Historical Park was one of many "places of refuge"—sites where lawbreakers could find safety and pardon if they could reach there before being caught. There were many kapu, forbidden things, in ancient Hawaiʻi. Murder was kapu and so was touching a chief's possessions. Death was the penalty for breaking kapu, no exceptions, save reaching a place of refuge and receiving the pardon of the kahuna—the presiding priest.

The refuge on the shore near Hōnaunau is the most famous of these special places. It was also adjacent to the ancestral home of major chiefs. A huge wall—1,000 feet long, 10 feet high, and 17 feet wide—built of close-fitting blocks of lava separates the Puʻuhonua from the chief's home. This amazing structure built around 1550 still stands. One of the largest lava blocks is estimated to weigh more than five tons. Besides the historic structures, the sea-breeze, and the shady coconut grove, visitors can also enjoy seeing artisans carving koa canoes and pounding tapa cloth.

Puʻukoholā Heiau National Historic Site preserves a massive temple platform of stones built on the order of Kamehameha, the chief who conquered the islands into a single kingdom. Dedicated to his war god, Kū, the great temple was built in 1790-1791 of water-worn lava rocks from Pololū Valley, 20 miles north of the site. A human chain of workers passed the heavy stones from hand to hand.

Kaloko-Honokōhau National Historical Park is a shoreline park just north of Kailua-Kona that was once the site of an ancient Hawaiian settlement. Tidal fishponds connected to the sea, house platforms, a hōlua slide, and petroglyphs are among the remains that can be seen here. The hōlua, a wooden sled built to slide on smooth stones, provided a once popular sport. Hard to believe? Think about skim boards, skateboards, and snow boards—all popular ways today to race down a hill. Fun, but safer just to watch.

FOR MORE INFORMATION

NATIONAL PARKS ON THE INTERNET:
www.nps.gov

HAWAI'I VOLCANOES NATIONAL PARK
PO Box 52
Hawai'i National Park, HI 96718-0052
(808) 985-6000
www.nps.gov/havo

HAWAI'I NATURAL HISTORY
ASSOCIATION
PO Box 74
Hawai'i National Park, HI 96718
(808) 985-6051

ERUPTION INFORMATION:
(808) 985-6000

WEATHER CONDITIONS:
(808) 985-6000

HAWAIIAN VOLCANO OBSERVA-
TORY
http://hvo.wr.usgs.gov

HAWAIIAN NATIVE PLANTS
www.botany.hawaii.edu/faculty/
carr/default.htm

POLYNESIAN VOYAGING
SOCIETY
http://pvs.hawaii.org

LODGING INSIDE THE PARK

VOLCANO HOUSE
PO Box 53
Hawai'i Volcanoes National Park, HI
96718
(808) 967-7321
(808) 967-8429 (fax)

CAMPING INSIDE THE PARK

NĀMAKANI PAIO CAMP-
GROUND: No reservations available—first come, first served.

OTHER REGIONAL SITES

HALEAKALĀ NATIONAL PARK (Maui)
PO Box 369
Makawao, Maui, HI 96768
(808) 572-4400
www.nps.gov/hale

HAWAI'I STATE PARKS
Dept. of Land and Natural Resources
Kalanimoku Bldg., 1151 Punchbowl Street
Honolulu, HI 96813
(808) 587-0300
www.hawaii.gov/dlnr/

KALAUPAPA NATIONAL HISTORICAL PARK
PO Box 2222
Kalaupapa, Molokai, HI 96742
(808) 567-6802
www.nps.gov/kala

KALOKO-HONOKŌHAU NATIONAL HIST. PARK
Located in Kailua-Kona, HI
Write to: 73-4786 Kanalani Street, Suite 14

Kailua-Kona, HI 96740
(808) 329-6881 (ext. 3 for HQ, ext.1 for message)
www.nps.gov/kaho

PU'UHONUA O HŌNAUNAU NAT'L. HIST. PARK
Located in Hōnaunau, HI
Write to: PO Box 129
Hōnaunau, HI 96726
(808) 328-2326 (HQ), 328-2288 (Visitor Info)
www.nps.gov/puho

PU'UKOHOLĀ HEIAU NATIONAL HISTORIC SITE
Located in Kawaihae, HI
Write to: PO Box 44340
Kawaihae, HI 96743
(808) 882-7218 (HQ)
www.nps.gov/puhe

USS ARIZONA MEMORIAL
1 Arizona Memorial Place
Honolulu, HI
(808) 422-0561
www.nps.gov/usar

SUGGESTED READING

Babb, Janet. *HAWAI'I VOLCANOES: THE STORY BEHIND THE SCENERY*. Las Vegas, NV: KC Publications. 1999.

Carlquist, Sherwin. *HAWAII—A NATURAL HISTORY*. Kauai, HI: Pacific Tropical Botanical Garden. 1992.

Cox, Halley. *HAWAIIAN PETRO-GLYPHS:* Honolulu, HI: Bishop Museum Press. 1995.

Daws, Gavan. *SHOAL OF TIME:* Honolulu, HI: University of Hawai'i Press, 1989.

Decker, Barbara and Robert Decker. *ROAD GUIDE TO HAWAII VOLCANOES NATIONAL PARK.* Mariposa, CA: Double Decker Press. Fourth Edition. 1997.

Decker, Robert and Barbara Decker. *VOLCANOES IN AMERICA'S NATIONAL PARKS*. Hong Kong: Odyssey Publications. 2001.

Hazlett, Richard W. and D.W. Hyndman. *ROADSIDE GEOL-OGY OF HAWAII*. Missoula, MT: Mountain Press. 1991.

Heliker, Christina and Dorian Weisel. *KILAUEA: THE NEWEST LAND ON EARTH*. Honolulu, HI: Island Heritage Publishing. 1996

Juvik, Sonia P. and James O. Juvik.. *ATLAS OF HAWAI'I*, Third Edition. Honolulu, HI: University of Hawai'i Press. 1998.

Kirch, Patrick V. *FEATHERED GODS AND FISH HOOKS*. Honolulu, HI: University of Hawai'i Press. 1998.

Pratt, H. Douglas. *POCKET GUIDE TO HAWAI'I'S BIRDS*. Honolulu, HI: Mutual Publishing. 1996.

Stone, Charles P. and Linda W. Pratt. *HAWAI'I'S PLANTS AND ANIMALS*. Hawai'i National Park: Hawai'i Natural History Associa-tion.1994.

Wright, Thomas L., Taeko Jane Takahashi, and J.D. Griggs. *HAWAI'I VOLCANO WATCH*. Honolulu: University of Hawai'i Press. 1992.

ABOVE: Lava bursting as it enters the sea near Kamoamoa. PHOTO© G. BRAD LEWIS

PRODUCTION CREDITS

Publisher: Jeff D. Nicholas
Authors: Barbara and Robert Decker
Production Assistant: Marcia Huskey
Illustrations: Darlece Cleveland
Printing Coordination: Sung In Printing America

ISBN 1-58071-043-3 (Cloth), 1-58071-044-1 (Paper)
©2002 Panorama International Productions, Inc.

SIERRA PRESS

4988 Gold Leaf Drive, Mariposa, CA 95338
(209) 966-5071, 966-5073 (Fax)
e-mail: siepress@yosemite.net

SIERRA PRESS

VISIT OUR WEBSITE AT:
www.nationalparksusa.com

BELOW
Hāpu'u (tree ferns) and 'ōhi'a lehua near Nāhuku (Thurston Lava Tube). PHOTO© JEFF D. NICHOLAS
RIGHT
Lava from Kīlauea flowing into the Pacific Ocean.
PHOTO© G. BRAD LEWIS
OPPOSITE
Hawai'i Volcanoes National Park Map.
ILLUSTRATION BY DARLECE CLEVELAND
BACK COVER
Ropy pāhoehoe lava, Pali Uli.
PHOTO© FRED HIRSCHMANN
BACK COVER (INSET)
'Ama'u fern detail. PHOTO© G. BRAD LEWIS